Amelia Simmons

American Cookery

✤ ✤

A.R.
Shephard
& co.

Published by A.R. Shephard & Co.

ISBN: 978-1-62654-196-2

Printed and bound in the United States of America

AMERICAN COOKERY,

OR THE ART OF DRESSING

VIANDS, FISH, POULTRY and VEGETABLES,

AND THE BEST MODES OF MAKING

PASTES, PUFFS, PIES, TARTS, PUDDINGS, CUSTARDS AND PRESERVES,

AND ALL KINDS OF

CAKES,

FROM THE IMPERIAL PLUMB TO PLAIN CAKE.

ADAPTED TO THIS COUNTRY,

AND ALL GRADES OF LIFE.

By Amelia Simmons,

AN AMERICAN ORPHAN.

PUBLISHED ACCORDING TO ACT OF CONGRESS.

HARTFORD

PRINTED BY HUDSON & GOODWIN.

FOR THE AUTHOR.

1796

PREFACE.

✦✦✦✦✦✦✦✦✦✦✦✦✦

AS this treatife is calculated for the improvement of the rifing generation of *Females* in America, the Lady of fafhion and fortune will not be difpleafed, if many hints are fuggefted for the more general and univerfal knowledge of thofe females in this country, who by the lofs of their parents, or other unfortunate circumftances, are reduced to the neceffity of going into families in the line of domeftics, or taking refuge with their friends or relations, and doing thofe things which are really effential to the perfecting them as good wives, and ufeful members of fociety. The orphan, tho' left to the care of virtuous guardians, will find it effentially neceffary to have an opinion and determination of her own. The world, and the fafhion thereof, is fo variable, that old people cannot accommodate themfelves to the various changes and fafhions which daily occur; *they* will adhere to the fafhion of *their* day, and will not furrender their attachments to the *good old way*—while the young and the gay, bend and conform readily to the tafte of the times, and fancy of the hour. By having an opinion and determination, I would not be underftood to mean an obftinate perfeverance in trifles, which borders on obftinacy—by no means, but only an adherence to thofe rules and maxims which have ftood the teft of ages, and will forever eftablifh the *female character*, a virtuous character—altho' they conform to the ruling tafte of the age in cookery, drefs, language, manners, &c.

PREFACE.

It muſt ever remain a check upon the poor ſolita-ry orphan, that while thoſe females who have pa-rents, or brothers, or riches, to defend their indiſ-cretions, that the orphan muſt depend ſolely upon *character*. How immenſely important, therefore, that every action, every word, every thought, be re-gulated by the ſtricteſt purity, and that every move-ment meet the approbation of the good and wiſe.

The candor of the American Ladies is ſolicitouſly intreated by the Authoreſs, as ſhe is circumſcribed in her knowledge, this being an original work in this country. Should any future editions appear, ſhe hopes to render it more valuable.

DIRECTIONS for CATERING, or the procuring the beſt VIANDS, FISH, &c.

How to chooſe Fleſh.

BEEF. The large ſtall fed ox beef is the beſt, it has a coarſe open grain, and oily ſmoothneſs ; dent it with your finger and it will immediately riſe again ; if old, it will be rough and ſpungy, and the dent remain.

Cow Beef is leſs boned, and generally more tender and juicy than the ox, in America, which is uſed to labor.

Of almoſt every ſpecies of Animals, Birds and Fiſhes, the female is the tendereſt, the richeſt flavour'd, and among poultry the ſooneſt fatened.

Mutton, graſs-fed, is good two or three years old.

Lamb, if under ſix months is rich, and no danger of impoſition ; it may be known by its ſize, in diſtinguiſhing either.

Veal, is ſoon loſt—great care therefore is neceſſary in purchaſing. Veal bro't to market in panniers, or in carriages, is to be prefered to that bro't in bags, and flouncing on a ſweaty horſe.

Pork, is known by its ſize, and whether properly fattened by its appearance.

To make the beſt Bacon.

To each ham put one ounce ſaltpetre, one pint bay ſalt, one pint molaſſes, ſhake together 6 or 8 weeks, or when a large quantity is together, baſt them with the liquor every day ; when taken out to dry, fmoke three weeks with cobs or malt fumes. To every ham may be added a cheek, if you ftow away a barrel and not alter the compofition, fome add a fhoulder. For tranfportation or exportation, double the period of fmoaking.

Fifh, how to choofe the beft in market.

Salmon, the nobleft and richeft fifh taken in frefh water—the largeft are the beft. They are unlike almoft every other fifh, are ameliorated by being 3 or 4 days out of water, if kept from heat and the moon, which has much more injurious effect than the fun.

In all great fifh-markets, great fifh-mongers ftrictly examine the gills—if the bright rednefs is exchanged for a low brown, they are ftale ; but when live fifh are bro't flouncing into market, you have only to elect the kind moft agreeable to your palate and the feafon.

Shad, contrary to the generally received opinion are not fo much richer flavored, as they are harder when firft taken out of the water ; opinions vary refpecting them. I have tafted Shad thirty or forty miles from the place where caught, and really conceived that they had a richnefs of flavor, which did not appertain to thofe taken frefh and cooked immediately, and have proved both at the fame table, and the truth may reft here, that a Shad 36 or 48 hours out of water, may not cook fo hard and folid, and be efteemedfo elegant, yet give a higher relifhed flavor to the tafte.

Every fpecies generally of *falt water Fifh*, are beft frefh from the water, tho' the *Hannah Hill*, *Black Fifh*, *Lobfter*, *Oyfter*, *Flounder*, *Bafs*, *Cod*, *Haddock*, and *Eel*, with many others, may be tranfported by land many miles, find a good market, and retain a good relifh ; but as generally, live ones are bought firft, deceits are ufed to give them a frefhnefs of appearance, fuch as peppering the gills, wetting the fins and tails, and even painting the gills, or wetting with animal blood. Experience and attention will dictate the choice of the beſt. Freſh gills, full bright eyes, moiſt fins and tails, are denotements of their being freſh caught ; if they are ſoft, its certain they are ſtale, but if deceits are uſed, your ſmell muſt approve or denounce them, and be your ſafeſt guide.

Of all freſh water fiſh, there are none that require, or ſo well afford haſte in cookery, as the *Salmon Trout*, they are beſt when caught under a fall or cateract—from what philoſophical circumſtance is yet unſettled, yet true it is, that at the foot of a fall the waters are much colder than at the head ; Trout chooſe thoſe waters ; if taken from them and hurried into dreſs, they are genuinely good ; and take rank in point of ſuperiority of flavor, of moſt other fiſh.

Perch and Roach, are noble pan fiſh. the deeper the water from whence taken, the finer are their flavors ; if taken from ſhallow water, with muddy bottoms, they are impregnated therewith, and are unſavory.

Eels, though taken from muddy bottoms, are beſt to jump in the pan.

Moſt white or ſoft fiſh are beſt bloated, which is done by ſalting, peppering, and drying in the ſun, and in a chimney ; after 30 or 40 hours drying, are beſt broiled, and moiſtened with butter, &c.

Poultry—how to chooſe.

Having before ſtated that the female in almoſt every inſtance, is preferable to the male, and peculiarly ſo in the *Peacock*, which, tho' beautifully plumaged, is tough, hard, ſtringy, and untaſted, and even indelicious—while the *Pea Hen* is exactly otherwiſe, and the queen of all birds.

So alſo in a degree, *Turkey*.

Hen Turkey, is higher and richer flavor'd, eaſier fattened and plumper—they are no odds in market.

Dunghill Fowls, are from their frequent uſe, a tolerable proof of the former birds.

Chickens, of either kind are good, and the yellow leg'd the beſt, and their taſte the ſweeteſt.

Capons, if young are good, are known by ſhort ſpurs and ſmooth legs.

All birds are known, whether freſh killed or ſtale, by a tight vent in the former, and a looſe open vent if old or ſtale; their ſmell denotes their goodneſs; ſpeckled rough legs denote age, while ſmooth legs and combs prove them young.

A Gooſe, if young, the bill will be yellow, and will have but few hairs, the bones will crack eaſily; but if old, the contrary, the bill will be red, and the pads ſtill redder; the joints ſtiff and difficultly diſjointed; if young, otherwiſe; chooſe one not very fleſhy on the breaſt, but fat in the rump.

Ducks, are ſimilar to geeſe.

Wild Ducks, have redder pads, and ſmaller than the tame ones, otherwiſe are like the gooſe or tame duck, or to be choſen by the ſame rules.

Wood Cocks, ought to be thick, fat and fleſh firm, the noſe dry, and throat clear.

Snipes, if young and fat, have full veins under the wing, and are ſmall in the veins, otherwiſe like the Woodcock.

Partridges, if young, will have black bills, yellowiſh legs; if old, the legs look bluiſh; if old or ſtale, it may be perceived by ſmelling at their mouths.

Pigeons, young, have light red legs, and the fleſh of a colour, and prick eaſily—old have red legs, blackiſh in parts, more hairs, plumper and looſe vents—ſo alſo of grey or green Plover, Black Birds, Thraſh, Lark, and wild Fowl in general.

Hares, are white fleſh'd and flexible when new and freſh kill'd; if ſtale, their fleſh will have a blackiſh hue, like old pigions, if the cleft in her lip ſpread much, is wide and ragged, ſhe is old; the contrary when young.

Leveret, is like the Hare in every reſpect, that

some are obliged to search for the knob, or small bone on the fore leg or foot, to distinguish them.

Rabbits, the wild are the best, either are good and tender ; if old there will be much yellowish fat about the kidneys, the claws long, wool rough, and mixed with grey hairs ; if young the reverse. As to their being fresh, judge by the scent, they soon perish, if trap'd or shot, and left in pelt or undressed ; their taint is quicker than veal, and the most sickish in nature ; and will not, like beef or veal, be purged by fire.

The cultivation of Rabbits would be profitable in America, if the best methods were pursued—they are a very prolific and profitable animal—they are easily cultivated if properly attended, but not otherwise.— A Rabbit's borough, on which 3000 dollars may have been expended, might be very profitable ; but on the small scale they would be well near market towns—easier bred, and more valuable.

Butter—Tight, waxy, yellow Butter is better than white or crumbly, which soon becomes rancid and frowy. Go into the centre of balls or rolls to prove and judge it ; if in ferkin, the middle is to be preferred, as the sides are frequently distasted by the wood of the firkin—altho' oak and used for years. New pine tubs are ruinous to the butter. To have sweet butter in dog days, and thro' the vegetable seasons, send stone pots to honest, neat, and trusty dairy people, and procure it pack'd down in May, and let them be brought in in the night. or cool rainy morning, covered with a clean cloth wet in cold water, and partake of no heat from the horse, and set the pots in the coldest part of your cellar, or in the ice house.— Some say that May butter thus preserved, will go into the winter use, better than fall made butter.

Cheese—The red smooth moist coated, and tight pressed, square edged Cheese, are better than white coat, hard rinded, or bilged ; the inside should be yellow, and flavored to your taſte. Old ſhelves which have only been wiped down for years, are preferable to ſcoured and waſhed ſhelves. Deceits are uſed by ſalt-petering the out ſide, or colouring with hemlock, cocumberries, or ſafron, infuſed into the milk ; the taſte of either ſupercedes every poſſible evaſion.

Eggs—Clear, thin ſhell'd, longeſt oval and ſharp ends are beſt ; to aſcertain whether new or ſtale— hold to the light, if the white is clear, the yolk regu- larly in the centre, they are good—but if otherwiſe, they are ſtale. The beſt poſſible method of aſcer- taining, is to put them into water, if they lye on their bilge, they are *good* and *freſh*—if they bob up an end they are ſtale, and if they riſe they are addled, prov- ed, and of no uſe.

We proceed to ROOTS and VEGETABLES— *and the beſt cook cannot alter the firſt quality, they muſt be good, or the cook will be diſappointed.*

Potatoes, take rank for univerſal uſe, profit and ea- ſy acquirement. The ſmooth ſkin, known by the name of How's Potatoe, is the moſt mealy and richeſt flavor'd ; the yellow ruſticoat next beſt ; the red, and red ruſticoat are tolerable ; and the yellow Spaniſh have their value—thoſe cultivated from imported ſeed on ſandy or dry loomy lands, are beſt for table uſe ; tho' the red or either will produce more in rich, loomy, highly manured garden grounds ; new lands and a ſandy ſoil, afford the richeſt flavor'd ; and moſt mealy Potatoe much de- pends on the ground on which they grow—more on the ſpecies of Potatoes planted—and ſtill more from foreign ſeeds—and each may be known by attention to connoiſſeurs ; for a good potatoe comes up in ma- ny branches of cookery, as herein after preſcribed.— All potatoes ſhould be dug before the rainy ſeaſons in the fall, well dryed in the ſun, kept from froſt and dampneſs during the winter, in the ſpring removed from the cellar to a dry loft, and ſpread thin, and frequently ſtirred and dryed, or they will grow and be thereby injured for cookery.

A roaſt Potatoe is brought on with roaſt Beef, a Steake, a Chop, or Fricaſſee ; good boiled with a boiled diſh ; make an excellent ſtuffing for a turkey, water or wild fowl ; make a good pie, and a good ſtarch for many uſes. All potatoes run out, or depreciate in America ; a freſh importation of the Spaniſh might reſtore them to table uſe.

It would ſwell this treatiſe too much to ſay every thing that is uſeful, to prepare a good table, but I may be pardoned by obſerving, that the Iriſh have preſerved a genuine mealy rich Potatoe, for a century, which takes rank of any known in any other kingdom ; and I have heard that they renew their ſeed by planting and cultivating the *Seed Ball*, which grows on the tine. The manner of their managing it to keep up the excellency of that root, would better ſuit a treatiſe on agriculture and gardening than this—and be inſerted in a book which would be read by the farmer, inſtead of his amiable daughter. If no one treats on the ſubject, it may appear in the next edition.

Onions—The Medeira white is beſt in market, eſteemed ſofter flavored, and not ſo fiery, but the high red, round hard onions are the beſt ; if you conſult cheapneſs, the largeſt are beſt ; if you conſult taſte and ſoftneſs, the very ſmalleſt are the moſt delicate, and uſed at the firſt tables. Onions grow in the richeſt, higheſt cultivated ground, and better and better year after year, on the ſame ground.

Beets, grow on any ground, but beſt on loom, or light gravel grounds ; the *red* is the richeſt and beſt approved ; the *white* has a ſickiſh ſweetneſs, which is diſliked by many.

Parſnips, are a valuable root, cultivated beſt in rich old grounds, and doubly deep plowed, *late ſown*, they grow thrifty, and are not ſo prongy ; they may be kept any where and any how, ſo that they do not grow with heat, or are nipped with froft; if frofted, let them thaw in earth; they are richer flavored when plowed out of the ground in April, having ftood out during the winter, tho' they will not laft long after, and commonly more fticky and hard in the centre.

Carrots, are managed as it refpects plowing and rich ground, fimilarly to Parfnips. The yellow are better than the orange or red; middling fiz'd, that is, a foot long and two inches thick at the top end, are better than over grown ones; they are cultivated beft with onions, fowed very thin, and mixed with other feeds, while young or fix weeks after fown, efpecially if with onions on true onion ground. They are good with veal cookery, rich in foups, excellent with hafh, in May and June.

Garlicks, tho' ufed by the French, are better a-dapted to the ufes of medicine than cookery.

Afparagus—The mode of cultivation belongs to gardening; your bufinefs is only to cut and drefs, the largeft is beft, the growth of a day fufficient, fix inches long, and cut juft above the ground; many cut below the furface, under an idea of getting tender fhoots, and preferving the bed; but it enfeebles the root: dig round it and it will be wet with the juices—but if cut above ground, and juft as the dew is going off, the fun will either reduce the juice, or fend it back to nourifh the root—its an excellent vegetable.

Parfley, of the three kinds, the thickeft and branch-ieft is the beft, is fown among onions, or in a bed by itfelf, may be dryed for winter ufe; tho' a method which I have experienced is much better—In September I dig my roots, procure an old thin ftave dry cafk, bore holes an inch diameter in every ftave, 6 inches afunder round the cafk, and up to the top—take firft a half bufhel of rich garden mold and put into the cafk, then run the roots through the ftaves, leaving the branches outfide, prefs the earth tight a-bout the root within, and thus continue on thro' the respective stories, till the cask is full ; it being filled, run an iron bar thro' the center of the dirt in the cask, and fill with water, let stand on the south and east side of a building till frosty night, then remove it, (by flinging a rope round the cask) into the cellar; where, during the winter, I clip with my scissars the fresh parsley, which my neighbors or myself have occasion for ; and in the spring transplant the roots in the bed in the garden, or in any unused corner— or let stand upon the wharf, or the wash shed. Its an useful mode of cultivation, and a pleasurably tasted herb, and much used in garnishing viands.

Raddish, *Salmon* coloured is the best, *purple* next best—*white*—*turnip*—each are produced from southern seeds, annually. They grow thriftiest sown among onions. The turnip Raddish will last well through the winter.

Artichokes—The Jerusalem is best, are cultivated like potatoes, (tho' their stocks grow 7 feet high) and may be preserved like the turnip raddish, or pickled— they like,

Horse Raddish, once in the garden, can scarcely ever be totally eradicated ; plowing or digging them up with that view, seems at times rather to increase and spread them.

Cucumbers, are of many kinds ; the prickly is best for pickles, but generally bitter ; the white is difficult to raise and tender ; choose the bright green, smooth and proper sized.

Melons—The Water Melons is cultivated on sandy soils only, above latitude 41 1-2, if a stratum of land be dug from a well, it will bring the first year good Water Melons ; the red cored are highest flavored ; a hard rine proves them ripe.

Muskmelons, are various, the rough skinned is best to eat ; the short, round, fair skinn'd, is best for Mangoes.

Lettuce, is of various kinds ; the purple spotted

leaf is generally the tenderest, and free from bitter—
Your taste must guide your market.

Cabbage, requires a page, they are so multifarious.
Note, all Cabbages have a higher relish that grow on
new unmanured grounds ; if grown in an old town
and on old gardens, they have a rankness, which at
times, may be perceived by a fresh air traveller. This
observation has been experienced for years—that Cabbages require new ground, more than Turnips.

Th. Low Dutch, only will do in old gardens.

The *Early Yorkshire*, must have rich soils, they will
not answer for winter, they are easily cultivated, and
frequently bro't to market in the fall. but will not
last the winter.

The *Green Savoy*, with the richest crinkles, is fine
and tender ; and altho' they do not head like the
Dutch or Yorkshire, yet the tenderness of the out
leaves is a counterpoise, it will last thro' the winter,
and are high flavored.

The *Yellow Savoy*, takes next rank, but will not
last so long ; all Cabbages will mix, and participate
of other species, like Indian Corn ; they are cul d,
belt in pl nts ; and a true gardener will, in the plant
describe those which will head, and which will not.
This is new, but a fact.

The gradations in the Savoy Cabbage are discerned
by the leaf ; the richest and most scollup'd, and crink-
led, and thickest Green Savoy, falls little short of a
Colliflour.

The red and redest small tight heads, are best for
slaw, it will not boil well, comes out black or blue,
and tinges other things with which it is boiled.

B E A N S.

The Clabboard Bean, is easiest cultivated and col-
lected, are good for string beans, will shell—must be
poled.

The Windsor Bean, is an earlier, good string, or
shell Bean.

Crambury Bean, is rich, but not univerfally approved equal to the other two.

Froft Bean, is good only to fhell.

Six Weeks Bean, is a yellowifh Bean, and early bro't forward, and tolerable.

Lazy Bean, is tough, and needs no pole.

Englifh Bean, what *they* denominate the *Horfe Bean,* is mealy when young, is profitable, eafily cultivated, and may be grown on worn out grounds ; as they may be raifed by boys, I cannot but recommend the more extenfive cultivation of them.

The fmall White Bean, is beft for winter ufe, and excellent.

Calivanfe, are run out, a yellow fmall bufh, a black fpeck or eye, are tough and taftelefs, and little worth in cookery, and fcarcely bear exportation.

Peas—Green Peas.

The Crown Imperial, takes rank in point of flavor, they bloffom, purple and white on the top of the vines, will run from three to five feet high, fhould be fet in light fandy foil only, or they run too much to vines.

The Crown Pea, is fecond in richnefs of flavor.

The Rondeheval, is large and bitterifh.

Early Carlton, is produced firft in the feafon— good.

Marrow Fats, green, yellow, and is large, eafily cultivated, not equal to others.

Sugar Pea, needs no bufh, the pods are tender and good to eat, eafily cultivated.

Spanifh Manratto, is a rich Pea, requires a ftrong high bufh.

All Peas fhould be picked *carefully* from the vines as foon as dew is off, fhelled and cleaned without water, and boiled immediately ; they are thus the richeft flavored.

Herbs, ufeful in Cookery.

Thyme, is good in foups and ftuffings.

Sweet Marjoram, is ufed in Turkeys.

Summer Savory, ditto, and in Saufages and falted Beef, and legs of Pork.

Sage, is ufed in Cheefe and Pork, but not generally approved.

Parfley, good in *foups*, and to *garnifh roaft Beef*, excellent with bread and butter in the fpring.

Penny Royal, is a high aromatic, altho' a fpontaneous herb in old ploughed fields, yet might be more generally cultivated in gardens, and ufed in cookery and medicines.

Sweet Thyme, is moft ufeful and beft approved in cookery.

FRUITS.

Pears, There are many different kinds ; but the large Bell Pear, fometimes called the Pound Pear, the yelloweft is the beft, and in the fame town they differ effentially.

Hard Winter Pear, are innumerable in their qualities, are good in fauces, and baked.

Harveft and *Summer Pear* are a tolerable defert, are much improved in this country, as all other fruits are by grafting and innoculation.

Apples, are ftill more various, yet rigidly retain their own fpecies, and are highly ufeful in families, and ought to be more univerfally cultivated, excepting in the compacteft cities. There is not a fingle family but might fet a tree in fome otherwife ufelefs fpot, which might ferve the two fold ufe of fhade and fruit ; on which 12 or 14 kinds of fruit trees might eafily be engrafted, and effentiallypreferve the orchard from the intrufions of boys, &c. which is too common in America. If the boy who thus planted a tree, and guarded and protected it in a ufelefs corner, and carefully engrafted different fruits, was to be indulged free accefs into orchards, whilft the neglectful boy was prohibited—how many millions of fruit trees would fpring into growth—and what a faving to the union. The net faving would in time extinguifh the public debt, and enrich our cookery.

Currants, are eafily grown from fhoots trimmed off from old bunches, and fet carelefsly in the ground; they flourifh on all foils, and make good jellies—their cultivation ought to be encouraged.

Black Currants, may be cultivated—but until they can be dryed, and until fugars are propagated, they are in a degree unprofitable.

Grapes, are natural to the climate; grow fpontaneoufly in every ftate in the union, and ten degrees north of the line of the union. The *Madeira, Lifbon* and *Malaga* Grapes, are cultivated in gardens in this country, and are a rich treat or defert. Trifling attention only is neceffary for their ample growth.

Having pointed out the *beft methods of judging of the qualities of Viands, Poultry, Fifh, Vegetables, &c.* We now prefent the beft approved methods of DRESSING and COOKING them; and to fuit all taftes, prefent the following

RECEIPTS.

To Roaft Beef.

THE general rules are, to have a brifk hot fire, to hang down rather than to fpit, to bafte with falt and water, and one quarter of an hour to every pound of beef, tho' tender beef will require lefs, while old tough beef will require more roafting; pricking with a fork will determine you whether done or not; rare done is the healthieft and the tafte of this age.

Roaft Mutton.

If a breaft let it be cauled, if a leg, ftuffed or not, let it be done more gently than beef, and done more; the chine, faddle or leg require more fire and longer time than the breaft, &c. Garnifh with fcraped horfe radifh, and ferve with potatoes, beans, colliflowers, water-creffes, or boiled onion, caper fauce, mafhed turnip, or lettuce.

Roaſt Veal.

As it is more tender than beef or mutton, and eaſily ſcorched, paper it, eſpecially the fat parts, lay it ſome diſtance from the fire a while to heat gently, baſte it well ; a 15 pound piece requires one hour and a quarter roaſting; garniſh with green-parſley and ſliced lemon.

Roaſt Lamb.

Lay down to a clear good fire that will not want ſtirring or altering, baſte with butter, duſt on flour, baſte with the dripping, and before you take it up, add more butter and ſprinkle on a little ſalt and parſly ſhred fine ; ſend to table with a nice ſallad, green peas, freſh beans, or a colliflower, or aſparagus.

To ſtuff a Turkey.

Grate a wheat loaf, one quarter of a pound butter, one quarter of a pound ſalt pork, finely chopped, 2 eggs, a little ſweet marjoram, ſummer ſavory, parſley and ſage, pepper and ſalt (if the pork be not ſufficient,) fill the bird and ſew up.

The ſame will anſwer for all Wild Fowl.

Water Fowls require onions.

The ſame ingredients ſtuff a *leg of Veal*, *freſh Pork* or a *loin of Veal.*

To ſtuff and roaſt a Turkcy, or Fowl.

One pound ſoft wheat bread, 3 ounces beef ſuet, 3 eggs, a little ſweet thyme, ſweet marjoram, pepper and ſalt, and ſome add a gill of wine ; fill the bird therewith and ſew up, hang down to a ſteady ſolid fire, baſting frequently with ſalt and water, and roaſt until a ſteam emits from the breaſt, put one third of a pound of butter into the gravy, duſt flour over the bird and baſte with the gravy ; ſerve up with boiled onions and cramberry-ſauce, mangoes, pickles or celery.

2. Others omit the ſweet herbs, and add parſley done with potatoes.

3. Boil and maſh 3 pints potatoes, wet them with butter, add ſweet herbs, pepper, ſalt, fill and roaſt as above.

To stuff and roast a Goslin.

Boil the inwards tender, chop them fine, put double quantity of grated bread, 4 ounces butter, pepper, salt, (and sweet herbs if you like) 2 eggs moulded into the stuffing, parboil 4 onions and chop them into the stuffing, add wine, and roast the bird.

The above is a good stuffing for every kind of Water Fowl, which requires onion sauce.

To smother a Fowl in Oysters.

Fill the bird with dry Oysters, and sew up and boil in water just sufficient to cover the bird, salt and season to your taste—when done tender, put into a deep dish and pour over it a pint of stewed oysters, well buttered and peppered, garnish a turkey with sprigs of parsley or leaves of cellery : a fowl is best with a parsley sauce.

To stuff a Leg of Veal.

Take one pound of veal, half pound pork (salted,) one pound grated bread, chop all very fine, with a handful of green parsley, pepper it, add 3 ounces butter and 3 eggs, (and sweet herbs if you like them,) cut the leg round like a ham and stab it full of holes, and fill in all the stuffing ; then salt and pepper the leg and dust on some flour ; if baked in an oven, put into a sauce pan with a little water, if potted, lay some scewers at the bottom of the pot, put in a little water and lay the leg on the scewers, with a gentle fire render it tender, (frequently adding water,) when done take out the leg, put butter in the pot and brown the leg, the gravy in a separate vessel must be thickened and buttered and a spoonful of ketchup added.

To stuff a leg of Pork to bake or roast.

Corn the leg 48 hours and stuff with sausage meat and bake in a hot oven two hours and an half or roast.

To alamode a round of Beef.

To a 14 or 16 pound round of beef, put one ounce salt-petre, 48 hours after stuff it with the fol-

lowing : one and half pound beef, one pound falt
pork, two pound grated bread, chop all fine and rub
in half pound butter, falt, pepper and cayenne, fum-
mer favory, thyme ; lay it on fcewers in a large pot,
over 3 pints hot water (which it muft occafionally
be fupplied with,) the fteam of which in 4 or 5 hours
will render the round tender if over a moderate fire;
when tender, take away the gravy and thicken with
flour and butter, and boil, brown the round with butter and flour, adding ketchup and wine to your tafte.

To alamode a round.

Take fat pork cut in flices or mince, feafon it with
pepper, falt, fweet marjoram and thyme, cloves,
mace and nutmeg, make holes in the beef and ftuff
it the night before cooked ; put fome bones acrofs
the bottom of the pot to keep from burning, put in
one quart Claret wine, one quart water and one onion ; lay the round on the bones, cover clofe and
ftop it round the top with dough ; hang on in the
morning and ftew gently two hours ; turn it, and
ftop tight and ftew two hours more ; when done tender, grate a cruft of bread on the top and brown it
before the fire ; fcum the gravy and ferve in a butter
boat, ferve it with the refidue of the gravy in the
difh.

To Drefs a Turtle.

Fill a boiler or kettle, with a quantity of water fufficient to fcald the callapach and Callapee, the fins, &c.
and about 9 o'clock hang up your Turtle by the
hind fins, cut of the head and fave the blood, take a
fharp pointed knife and feparate the callapach from
the callapee, or the back from the belly part, down
to the fhoulders, fo as to come at the entrails which
take out, and clean them, as you would thofe of any
other animal, and throw them into a tub of clean water, taking great care not to break the gall, but to
cut it off from the liver and throw it away, then feparate each diftinctly and put the guts into another
veffel, open them with a fmall pen-knife end to end,

wash them clean, and draw them through a woolen cloth, in warm water, to clear away the slime and then put them in clean cold water till they are used with the other part of the entrails, which must be cut up small to be mixed in the baking dishes with the meat ; this done, separate the back and belly pieces, entirely cutting away the fore fins by the upper joint, which scald; peal off the loose skin and cut them into small pieces, laying them by themselves, either in another vessel, or on the table, ready to be seasoned ; then cut off the meat from the belly part, and clean the back from the lungs, kidneys, &c. and that meat cut into pieces as small as a walnut, laying it likewise by itself ; after this you are to scald the back and belly pieces, pulling off the shell from the back, and the yellow skin from the belly, when all will be white and clean, and with the kitchen cleaver cut those up likewise into pieces about the bigness or breadth of a card ; put those pieces into clean cold water, wash them and place them in a heap on the table, so that each part may lay by itself; the meat being thus prepared and laid separate for seasoning ; mix two third parts of salt or rather more, and one third part of cyanne pepper, black pepper, and a nutmeg, and mace pounded fine, and mixt all together ; the quantity, to be proportioned to the size of the Turtle, so that in each dish there may be about three spoonfuls of seasoning to every twelve pound of meat ; your meat being thus seasoned, get some sweet herbs, such as thyme, savory, &c. let them be dryed and rub'd fine, and having provided some deep dishes to bake it in, which should be of the common brown ware, put in the coarsest part of the meat, put a quarter pound of butter at the bottom of each dish, and then put some of each of the several parcels of meat, so that the dishes may be all alike and have equal portions of the different parts of the Turtle, and between each laying of meat strew a little of the mixture of sweet herbs, fill your dishes within an inch an half, or two inches of the top ; boil the blood of the Turtle, and put into it, then lay on forcemeat balls made of veal, highly seasoned with the same seasoning as the Turtle; put in each dish a gill of Madeira Wine, and as much water as it will conveniently hold, then break over it five or six eggs to keep the meat from scorching at the top, and over that shake a handful of shread parsley, to make it look green, when done put your dishes into an oven made hot enough to bake bread, and in an hour and half, or two hours (according to the size of the dishes) it will be sufficiently done.

To dress a Calve's Head. Turtle fashion.

The head and feet being well scalded and cleaned, open the head, taking the brains, wash, pick and cleanse, salt and pepper and parsley them and put bye in a cloth; boil the head, feet and heartslet one and quarter, or one and half hour, sever out the bones, cut the skin and meat in slices, strain the liquor in which boiled and put by; clean the pot very clean or it will burn too, make a layer of the slices, which dust with a composition made of black pepper one spoon, of sweet herbs pulverized, two spoons (sweet marjoram and thyme are most approved) a tea spoon of cayenne, one pound butter, then dust with flour, then a layer of slices with slices of veal and seasoning till compleated, cover with the liquor, stew gently three quarters of an hour. To make the forced meat balls—take one and half pound veal, one pound grated bread, 4 ounces raw salt pork, mince and season with above and work with 3 whites into balls, one or one an half inch diameter, roll in flour, and fry in very hot butter till brown, then chop the brains fine and stir into the whole mess in the pot, put thereto, one third part of the fryed balls and a pint wine or less, when all is heated thro' take off and serve in tureens, laying the residue of the balls and hard boiled and pealed eggs into a dish, garnish with slices of lemon.

A Stew Pie.

Boil a shoulder of Veal, and cut up, salt, pepper,

and butter half pound, and flices of raw falt pork, make a layer of meat, and a layer of bifcuit, or bifcuit dough into a pot, cover clofe and ftew half an hour in three quarts of water only.

A *Sea Pie*.

Four pound of flour, one and half pound of butter rolled into pafte, wet with cold water, line the pot therewith, lay in fplit pigeons, turkey pies, veal, mutton or birds, with flices of pork, falt, pepper, and duft on flour, doing thus till the pot is full or your ingredients expended, add three pints water, cover tight with pafte, and ftew moderately two and half hours.

A *Chicken Pie*.

Pick and clean fix chickens, (without fcalding) take out their inwards and wafh the birds while whole, then joint the birds, falt and pepper the pieces and inwards. Roll one inch thick pafte No. 8 and cover a deep difh, and double at the rim or edge of the difh, put thereto a layer of chickens and a layer of thin flices of butter, till the chickens and one and a half pound butter are expended, which cover with a thick pafte; bake one and a half hour.

Or if your oven be poor, parboil the chickens with half a pound of butter, and put the pieces with the remaining one pound of butter, and half the gravy into the pafte, and while boiling, thicken the refidue of the gravy, and when the pie is drawn, open the cruft, and add the gravy.

Minced Pies. A Foot Pie.

Scald neets feet, and clean well, (grafs fed are beft) put them into a large veffel of cold water, which change daily during a week, then boil the feet till tender, and take away the bones, when cold, chop fine, to every four pound minced meat, add one pound of beef fuet, and four pound apple raw, and a little falt, chop all together very fine, add one quart of wine, two pound of ftoned raifins, one ounce of cinnamon, one ounce mace, and fweeten to your tafte; make ufe of pafte No. 3—bake three quarters of an hour.

Weeks after, when you have occafion to ufe them, carefully raife the top cruft, and with a round edg'd fpoon, collect the meat into a bafon, which warm with additional wine and fpices to the tafte of your circle, while the cruft is alfo warm'd like a hoe cake, put carefully together and ferve up, by this means you can have hot pies through the winter, and enrich'd fingly to your company.

Tongue Pie.

One pound neat's tongue, one pound apple, one third of a pound of Sugar, one quarter of a pound of butter, one pint of wine, one pound of raifins, or currants, (or half of each) half ounce of cinnamon and mace—bake in pafte No. 1, in proportion to fize.

Minced Pie of Beef.

Four pound boild beef, chopped fine, and falted ; fix pound of raw apple chopped alfo, one pound beef fuet, one quart of Wine or rich fweet cyder, one ounce mace, and cinnamon, a nutmeg, two pounds raifins, bake in pafte No. 3, three fourths ofan hour.

Obfervations.

All meat pies require a hotter and brifker oven than fruit pies, in good cookeries, all raifins fhould be ftoned.—As people differ in their taftes, they may alter to their wifhes. And as it is difficult to afcertain with precifion the fmall articles of fpicery ; every one may relifh as they like, and fuit their tafte.

Apple Pie.

Stew and ftrain the apples, to every three pints, grate the peal of a frefh lemon, add cinnamon, mace, rofe-water and fugar to your tafte—and bake in pafte No. 3.

Every fpecies of fruit fuch as peas, plums, rafberries, black berries may be only f eetned, without fpices—and bake in pafte No. 3.

Currant Pies.

Take green, full grown currants, and one third their quantity of fugar, proceeding as above.

A buttered apple Pie.

Pare, quarter and core tart apples, lay in paſte
No. 3, cover with the ſame ; bake half an hour,
when drawn, gently raiſe the top cruſt, add ſugar
butter, cinnamon, mace, wine or roſe-water q : ſ:

PUDDINGS.
A Rice Pudding.

One quarter of a pound rice, a ſtick of cinnamon,
to a quart of milk (ſtirred often to keep from
burning) and boil quick, cool and add half a nutmeg,
4 ſpoons roſe-water, 8 eggs ; butter or puff paſte a
diſh and pour the above compoſition into it, and
bake one and half hour.

No. 2. Boil 6 ounces rice in a quart milk, on a ſlow
fire 'till tender, ſtir in one pound butter, interim
beet 14 eggs, add to the pudding when cold with ſugar, ſalt, roſe-water and ſpices to your taſte, adding
raiſins or currants, bake as No. 1.

No. 3. 8 ſpoons rice boiled in 2 quarts milk,
when cooled add 8 eggs, 6 ounces butter, wine, ſugar and ſpices, q: ſ: bake 2 hours.

No. 4. Boil in water half pound ground rice till
ſoft, add 2 quarts milk and ſcald, cool and add 8
eggs, 6 ounces butter, 1 pound raiſins, ſalt, cinnamon and a ſmall nutmeg, bake 2 hours.

No. 5. *A cheap one*, half pint rice, 2 quarts milk,
ſalt, butter, allſpice, put cold into a hot oven, bake
2 and half hours.

No. 6. Put 6 ounces rice into water, or milk and
water, let it ſwell or ſoak tender, then boil gently,
ſtirring in a little butter, when cool ſtir in a quart
cream, 6 or 8 eggs well beaten, and add cinnamon
nutmeg, and ſugar to your taſte, bake.

N. B. The mode of introducing the ingredients,
is a material point ; in all caſes where eggs are mentioned it is underſtood to be well beat ; whites and
yolks and the ſpices, fine and ſettled.

A Nice Indian Pudding.

No. 1. 3 pints scalded milk, 7 spoons fine Indian meal, stir well together while hot, let stand till cooled; add 7 eggs, half pound raisins, 4 ounces butter, spice and sugar, bake one and half hour.

No. 2. 3 pints scalded milk to one pint meal salted; cool, add 2 eggs, 4 ounces butter, sugar or molasses and spice q. s. it will require two and half hours baking.

No. 3. Salt a pint meal, wet with one quart milk, sweeten and put into a strong cloth, brass or bell metal vessel, stone or earthern pot, secure from wet and boil 12 hours.

A Sunderland Pudding.

Whip 6 eggs, half the whites, take half a nutmeg, one point cream and a little salt, 4 spoons fine flour, oil or butter pans, cups, or bowls, bake in a quick oven one hour. Eat with sweet sauce.

A Whitpot.

Cut half a loaf of bread in slices, pour thereon 2 quarts milk, 6 eggs, rose-water, nutmeg and half pound of sugar; put into a dish and cover with paste, No. 1. bake slow 1 hour.

A Bread Pudding.

One pound soft bread or biscuit soaked in one quart milk, run thro' a sieve or cullender, add 7 eggs, three quarters of a pound sugar, one quarter of a pound butter, nutmeg or cinnamon, one gill rose-water, one pound stoned raisins, half pint cream, bake three quarters of an hour, middling oven.

A Flour Pudding.

Seven eggs, one quarter of a pound of sugar, and a tea spoon of salt, beat and put to one quart milk, 5 spoons of flour, cinnamon and nutmeg to your taste, bake half an hour, and serve up with sweet sauce.

A boiled Flour Pudding.

One quart milk, 9 eggs, 7 spoons flour, a little salt, put into a strong cloth and boiled three quarters of an hour.

A Cream Almond Pudding.

Boil gently a little mace and half a nutmeg (grated) in a quart cream ; when cool, beat 8 yolks and 3 whites, ſtrain and mix with one ſpoon flour one quarter of a pound almonds ; ſettled, add one ſpoon roſe-water, and by degrees the cold cream and beat well together ; wet a thick cloth and flour it, and pour in the pudding, boil hard half an hour, take out, pour over it melted butter and ſugar.

An apple Pudding Dumplin.

Put into paſte, quartered apples, lye in a cloth and boil two hours, ſerve with ſweet ſauce.

Pears, Plumbs, &c.

Are done the ſame way.

Potatoe Pudding.   Baked.

No. 1.   One pound boiled potatoes, one pound ſugar, half a pound butter, 10 eggs.

No. 2.   One pound boiled potatoes, maſhed, three quarters of a pound butter, 3 gills milk or cream, the juice of one lemon and the peal grated, half a pound ſugar, half nutmeg, 7 eggs (taking out 3 whites,) 2 ſpoons roſe-water.

Apple Pudding.

One pound apple ſifted, one pound ſugar, 9 eggs, one quarter of a pound butter, one quart ſweet cream, one gill roſe-water, a cinnamon, a green lemon peal grated (if ſweet apples,) add the juice of half a lemon, put on to paſte No. 7.   Currants, raiſins and citron ſome add, but good without them.

Carrot Pudding.

A coffee cup full of boiled and ſtrained carrots, 5 eggs, 2 ounces ſugar and butter each, cinnamon and roſe water to your taſte, baked in a deep diſh without paſte.

A Crookneck, or Winter Squaſh Pudding.

Core, boil and ſkin a good ſquaſh, and bruize it well ; take 6 large apples, pared, cored, and ſtewed tender, mix together ; add 6 or 7 ſpoonsful of dry bread or biſcuit, rendered fine as meal, half pint milk or cream, 2 spoons of rose-water, 2 do. wine, 5 or 6 eggs beaten and strained, nutmeg, salt and sugar to your taste, one spoon flour, beat all smartly together, bake.

The above is a good receipt for Pompkins, Potatoes or Yams, adding more moistening or milk and rose water, and to the two latter a few black or Lisbon currants, or dry whortleberries scattered in, will make it better.

Pompkin.

No. 1. One quart stewed and strained, 3 pints cream, 9 beaten eggs, sugar, mace, nutmeg and ginger, laid into paste No. 7 or 3, and with a dough spur, cross and chequer it, and baked in dishes three quarters of an hour.

No. 2. One quart of milk, 1 pint pompkin, 4 eggs, molasses, allspice and ginger in a crust, bake 1 hour.

Orange Pudding.

Put sixteen yolks with half a pound butter melted, grate in the rinds of two Seville oranges, beat in half pound of fine Sugar, add two spoons orange water, two of rose-water, one gill of wine, half pint cream, two naples biscuit or the crumbs of a fine loaf, or roll soaked in cream, mix all together, put it into rich puff-paste, which let be double round the edges of the dish ; bake like a custard.

A Lemon Pudding.

1. Grate the yellow of the peals of three lemons, then take two whole lemons, roll under your hand on the table till soft, taking care not to burst them, cut and squeeze them into the grated peals.

2. Take ten ounces soft wheat bread, and put a pint of scalded white wine thereto, let soak and put to No. 1.

3. Beat four whites and eight yolks, and put to above, adding three quarters of a pound of melted butter, (which let be very fresh and good) one pound fine sugar, beat all together till thorougly mixed.

4. Lay paste No. 7 or 9 on a dish, plate or saucers, and fill with above composition.

5. Bake near 1 hour, and when baked—stick on pieces of paste, cut with a jagging iron or a dough-spur to your fancy, baked lightly on a floured paper; garnished thus, they may be served hot or cold.

Puff Pastes for Tarts.

No. 1. Rub one pound of butter into one pound of flour, whip 2 whites and add with cold water and one yolk; make into paste, roll in in six or seven times one pound of butter, flowring it each roll. This is good for any small thing.

No. 2. Rub six pound of butter into fourteen pound of flour, eight eggs, add cold water, make a stiff paste.

No. 3. To any quantity of flour, rub in three fourths of it's weight of butter, (twelve eggs to a peck) rub in one third or half, and roll in the rest.

No. 4. Into two quarts flour (salted) and wet stiff with cold water roll in, in nine or ten times one and half pound of butter.

No. 5. One pound flour, three fourths of a pound of butter, beat well.

No. 6. To one pound of flour rub in one fourth of a pound of butter wet with three eggs and rolled in a half pound of butter.

A Paste for Sweet Meats.

No. 7. Rub one third of one pound of butter, and one pound of lard into two pound of flour, wet with four whites well beaten; water q : f : to make a paste, roll in the residue of shortning in ten or twelve rollings—bake quick.

No. 8. Rub in one and half pound of suet to six pounds of flour, and a spoon full of salt, wet with cream roll in, in six or eight times, two and half pounds of butter—good for a chicken or meat pie.

Royal Paste,

No. 9. Rub half a pound of butter into one pound of flour, four whites beat to a foam, add two yolks, two ounces of fine sugar; roll often, rubbing one third, and rolling two thirds of the butter is best; excellent for tarts and apple cakes.

CUSTARDS.

1. One pint cream sweetened to your taste, warmed hot; stir in sweet wine, till curdled, grate in cinnamon and nutmeg.

2. Sweeten a quart of milk, add nutmeg, wine, brandy, rose-water and six eggs; bake in tea cups or dishes, or boil in water, taking care that it don't boil into the cups.

3. Put a stick of cinnamon to one quart of milk, boil well, add six eggs, two spoons of rose-water—bake.

4. *Boiled Custard*—one pint of cream, two ounces of almonds, two spoons of rose-water, or orange flower water, some mace; boil thick, then stir in sweetning, and lade off into china cups, and serve up.

Rice Custard.

Boil a little mace, a quartered nutmeg in a quart of cream, add rice (well boiled) while boiling sweeten and flavor with orange or rose water, putting into cups or dishes, when cooled, set to serve up.

A Rich Custard.

Four eggs beat and put to one quart cream, sweetened to your taste, half a nutmeg, and a little cinnamon—baked.

A sick bed Custard.

Scald a quart milk, sweeten and salt a little, whip 3 eggs and stir in, bake on coals in a pewter vessel.

TARTS.

Apple Tarts.

Stew and strain the apples, add cinnamon, rose-water, wine and sugar to your taste, lay in paste, royal, squeeze thereon orange juice—bake gently.

Cramberries.

Stewed, strained and sweetened, put into paste No. 9, and baked gently.

Marmalade, laid into paste No. 1, baked gently.

Appricots, muft be neither pared, cut or ftoned, but put in whole, and fugar fifted over them, as above.

Orange or Lemon Tart.

Take 6 large lemons, rub them well in falt, put them into falt and water and let reft 2 days, change them daily in frefh water, 14 days, then cut flices and mince as fine as you can and boil them 2 or 3 hours till tender, then take 6 pippins, pare, quarter and core them, boil in 1 pint fair water till the pippins break, then put the half of the pippins, with all the liquor to the orange or lemon, and add one pound fugar, boil all together one quarter of an hour, put into a gallipot and fqueeze thereto a frefh orange, one fpoon of which, with a fpoon of the pulp of the pippin, laid into a thin royal pafte, laid into fmall fhallow pans or faucers, brufhed with melted butter, and fome fuperfine fugar fifted thereon, with a gentle baking, will be very good.

N. B. paftry pans, or faucers, muft be buttered lightly before the pafte is laid on. If glafs or China be ufed, have only a top cruft, you can garnifh with cut pafte, like a lemon pudding or ferve on pafte No. 7.

Goofeberry Tart.

Lay clean berries and fift over them fugar, then berries and fugar 'till a deep difh be filled, cover with pafte No. 9, and bake fome what more than other tarts.

Grapes, muft be cut in two and ftoned and done like a Goofeberry.

SYLLABUBS.

To make a fine Syllabub from the Cow.

Sweeten a quart of cyder with double refined fugar, grate nutmeg into it, then milk your cow into your liquor, when you have thus added what quantity of milk you think proper, pour half a pint or more, in proportion to the quantity of fyllabub you make, of the fweeteft cream you can get all over it.

A *Whipt Syllabub*.

Take two porringers of cream and one of white wine, grate in the skin of a lemon, take the whites of three eggs, sweeten it to your taste, then whip it with a whisk, take off the froth as it rises and put it into your syllabub glasses or pots , and they are fit for use.

To make a fine Cream.

Take a pint of cream, sweeten it to your pallate, grate a little nutmeg, put in a spoonful of orange flower water and rose water, and two sponfuls of wine; beat up four eggs and two whites, stir it all together one way over the fire till it is thick, have cups ready and pour it in.

Lemon Cream.

Take the juice of four large lemons, half a pint of water, a pound of double refined sugar beaten fine, the whites of seven eggs and the yolk of one beaten very well; mix altogether, strain it, set it on a gentle fire, stiring it all the while and skim it clean, put into it the peal of one lemon, when it is very hot, but not to boil; take out the lemon peal and pour it into china dishes.

Raspberry Cream.

Take a quart of thick sweet cream and boil it two or three wallops, then take it off the fire and strain some juices of raspberries into it to your taste, stir it a good while before you put your juice in, that it may be almost cold, when you put it to it, and afterwards stir it one way for almost a quarter of an hour; then sweeten it to your taste and when it is cold you may send it up.

Whipt Cream.

Take a quart of cream and the whites of 8 eggs beaten with half a pint of wine; mix it together and sweeten it to your taste with double refined sugar, you may perfume it (if you please) with musk or Amber gum tied in a rag and steeped a little in the cream, whip it up with a whisk and a bit of lemon peel tyed in the middle of the whisk, take off the froth with a spoon, and put into glasses.

A Trifle.

Fill a dish with biscuit finely broken, rusk and spiced cake, wet with wine, then pour a good boil'd custard, (not too thick) over the rusk, and put a syllabub over that; garnish with jelley and flowers.

CAKE.

Plumb Cake.

Mix one pound currants, one drachm nutmeg, mace and cinnamon each, a little salt, one pound of citron, orange peal candied, and almonds bleach'd, 6 pound of flour, (well dry'd) beat 21 eggs, and add with 1 quart new ale yeast, half pint of wine, 3 half pints of cream and raisins, q: s:

Plain Cake.

Nine pound of flour, 3 pound of sugar, 3 pound of butter, 1 quart emptins, 1 quart milk, 9 eggs, 1 ounce of spice, 1 gill of rose-water, 1 gill of wine.

Another.

Three quarters of a pound of sugar, 1 pound of butter, and 6 eggs work'd into 1 pound of flour.

A rich Cake.

Rub 2 pound of butter into 5 pound of flour, add 15 eggs (not much beaten) 1 pint of emptins, 1 pint of wine, kneed up stiff like biscuit, cover well and put by and let rise over night.

To 2 and a half pound raisins, add 1 gill brandy, to soak over night, or if new half an hour in the morning, add them with 1 gill rose-water and 2 and half pound of loaf sugar, 1 ounce cinnamon, work well and bake as loaf cake, No. 1.

Potatoe Cake.

Boil potatoes, peal and pound them, add yolks of eggs, wine and melted butter work with flour into paste, shape as you please, bake and pour over them melted butter, wine and sugar.

Johny Cake, or Hoe Cake.

Scald 1 pint of milk and put to 3 pints of indian meal, and half pint of flower—bake before the fire. Or scald with milk two thirds of the indian meal, or wet two thirds with boiling water, add salt, molasses and shortening, work up with cold water pretty stiff, and bake as above.

Indian Slapjack.

One quart of milk, 1 pint of indian meal, 4 eggs, 4 spoons of flour, little salt, beat together, baked on gridles, or fry in a dry pan, or baked in a pan which has been rub'd with suet, lard or butter.

Loaf Cakes.

No. 1. Rub 6 pound of sugar, 2 pound of lard, 3 pound of butter into 12 pound of flour, add 18 eggs, 1 quart of milk, 2 ounces of cinnamon, 2 small nutmegs, a tea cup of coriander seed, each pounded fine and sifted, add one pint of brandy, half a pint of wine, 6 pound of stoned raisins, 1 pint of emptins, first having dried your flour in the oven, dry and roll the sugar fine, rub your shortning and sugar half an hour, it will render the cake much whiter and lighter, heat the oven with dry wood, for 1 and a half hours, if large pans be used, it will then require 2 hours baking, and in proportion for smaller loaves. To frost it. Whip 6 whites, during the baking, add 3 pound of sifted loaf sugar and put on thick, as it comes hot from the oven. Some return the frosted loaf into the oven, it injures and yellows it, if the frosting be put on immediately it does best without being returned into the oven.

Another.

No. 2. Rub 4 pound of sugar, 3 and a half pound of shortning, (half butter and half lard) into 9 pound of flour, 1 dozen of eggs, 2 ounces of cinnamon, 1 pint of milk, 3 spoonfuls coriander seed, 3 gills of brandy, 1 gill of wine, 3 gills of emptins, 4 pounds of raisins.

Another.

No. 3. Six pound of flour, 3 of sugar, 2 and a half pound of shortning, (half butter, half lard) 6 eggs, 1 nutmeg, 1 ounce of cinnamon and 1 ounce of coriander seed, 1 pint of emptins, 2 gills brandy, 1 pint of milk and 3 pound of raisins.

Another.

No. 4. Five pound of flour, 2 pound of butter, 2 and a half pounds of loaf sugar, 2 and a half pounds of raisins, 15 eggs, 1 pint of wine, 1 pint of emptins, 1 ounce of cinnamon, 1 gill rose-water, 1 gill of brandy—baked like No. 1.

Another Plain cake.

No. 5. Two quarts milk, 3 pound of sugar, 3 pound of shortning, warmed hot, add a quart of sweet cyder, this curdle, add 18 eggs, allspice and orange to your taste, or fennel, carroway or coriander seeds ; put to 9 pounds of flour, 3 pints emptins, and bake well.

Cookies.

One pound sugar boiled slowly in half pint water, scum well and cool, add two tea spoons pearl ash dissolved in milk, then two and half pounds flour, rub in 4 ounces butter, and two large spoons of finely powdered coriander seed, wet with above ; make roles half an inch thick and cut to the shape you please ; bake fifteen or twenty minutes in a slack oven—good three weeks.

Another Christmas Cookey.

To three pound flour, sprinkle a tea cup of fine powdered coriander seed, rub in one pound butter, and one and half pound sugar, dissolve three tea spoonfuls of pearl ash in a tea cup of milk, kneed all together well, roll three quarters of an inch thick, and cut or stamp into shape and size you please, bake slowly fifteen or twenty minutes ; tho' hard and dry at first, if put into an earthern pot, and dry cellar, or damp room, they will be finer, softer and better when six months old.

Molasses Gingerbread.

One table spoon of cinnamon, some corian-
der or allspice, put to four tea spoons pearl ash, dissolved in half pint water, four pound flour, one quart
molasses, four ounces butter, (if in summer rub in
the butter, if in winter, warm the butter and molasses
and pour to the spiced flour,) knead well 'till stiff,
the more the better, the lighter and whiter it will be ;
bake brisk fifteen minutes ; don't scorch ; before it is
put in, wash it with whites and sugar beat together.

Gingerbread Cakes, or butter and sugar Gingerbread.

No. 1. Three pounds of flour, a grated nutmeg,
two ounces ginger, one pound sugar, three small
spoons pearl ash dissolved in cream, one pound butter, four eggs, knead it stiff, shape it to your fancy,
bake 15 minutes.

Soft Gingerbread to be baked in pans.

No. 2. Rub three pounds of sugar, two pounds of
butter, into four pounds of flour, add 20 eggs, 4 ounces ginger, 4 spoons rose water, bake as No. 1.

Butter drop do.

No. 3. Rub one quarter of a pound butter, one
pound sugar, sprinkled with mace, into one pound
and a quarter flour, add four eggs, one glass rose water, bake as No. 1.

Gingerbread.

No. 4. Three pound sugar, half pound butter,
quarter of a pound of ginger, one doz. eggs, one glass
rose water, rub into three pounds flour, bake as No. 1.

A cheap seed Cake.

Rub one pound sugar, half an ounce allspice into
four quarts flour, into which pour one pound butter,
melted in one pint milk, nine eggs, one gill emptins,
(carroway seed and currants, or raisins if you please)
make into two loaves, bake one and half hour.

Queens Cake.

Whip half pound butter to a cream, add 1 pound
sugar, ten eggs, one glass wine, half gill rose water,
and spices to your taste, all worked into one and a

quarter pound flour, put into pans, cover with paper, and bake in a quick well heat oven, 12 or 16 minutes.

Pound Cake.

One pound sugar, one pound butter, one pound flour, one pound or ten eggs, rose water one gill, spices to your taste; watch it well, it will bake in a slow oven in 15 minutes.

Another (called) Pound Cake.

Work three quarters of a pound butter, one pound of good sugar, 'till very white, whip ten whites to a foam, add the yolks and beat together, add one spoon rose water, 2 of brandy, and put the whole to one and and a quarter of a pound flour, if yet too soft add flour and bake slowly.

Soft Cakes in little pans.

One and half pound sugar, half pound butter, rubbed into two pounds flour, add one glass wine, one do. rose water, 18 eggs and a nutmeg.

A light Cake to bake in small cups.

Half a pound sugar, half a pound butter, rubbed into two pounds flour, one glass wine, one do rose water, two do. emptins, a nutmeg, cinnamon and currants.

Shrewsbury Cake.

One pound butter, three quarters of a pound sugar, a little mace, four eggs mixed and beat with your hand, till very light, put the composition to one pound flour, roll into small cakes—bake with a light oven.

N. B. In all cases where spices are named, it is supposed that they be pounded fine and sifted; sugar must be dryed and rolled fine; flour, dryed in an oven; eggs well beat or whipped into a raging foam.

Diet Bread.

One pound sugar, 9 eggs, beat for an hour, add to 14 ounces flour, spoonful rose water, one do. cinnamon or coriander, bake quick.

R U S K.—*To make.*

No. 1. Rub in half pound sugar, half pound butter, to four pound flour, add pint milk, pint emptins; when risen well, bake in pans ten minutes, fast.

No. 2. One pound sugar, one pound butter, six eggs, rubbed into 5 pounds flour, one quart emptins and wet with milk, sufficient to bake, as above.

No. 3. One pound sugar, one pound butter, rubbed into 6 or 8 pounds of flour, 12 eggs, one pint emptins, wet soft with milk, and bake.

No. 4. P. C. rusk. Put fifteen eggs to 4 pounds flour and make into large biscuit; and bake double, or one top of another.

No. 5. One pint milk, one pint emptins, to be laid over night in spunge, in morning, melt three quarters of a pound butter, one pound sugar, in another pint of milk, add luke warm, and beat till it rise well.

No. 6 Three quarters of a pound butter, one pound sugar, 12 eggs, one quart milk, put as much flour as they will wet, a spoon of cinnamon, gill emptins, let it stand till very puffy or light; roll into small cakes and let it stand on oiled tins while the oven is heating, bake 15 minutes in a quick oven, then wash the top with sugar and whites, while hot.

Biscuit.

One pound flour, one ounce butter, one egg, wet with milk and break while oven is heating, and in the same proportion.

Butter Biscuit.

One pint each milk and emptins, laid into flour, in sponge; next morning add one pound butter melted, not hot, and knead into as much flower as will with another pint of warmed milk, be of a sufficient consistance to make soft—some melt the butter in the milk.

A Butter Drop.

Four yolks, two whites, one pound flour, a quarter of a pound butter, one pound sugar, two spoons rose water, a little mace, baked in tin pans.

PRESERVES.

For preserving Quinces.

Take a peck of Quinces, pare them, take out the core with a sharp knife, if you wish to have them whole; boil parings and cores with two pound frost grapes, in 3 quarts water, boil the liquor an hour and an half, or till it is thick, strain it through a coarse hair sieve, add one and a quarter pound sugar to every pound of quince; put the sugar into the sirrup, scald and scim it till it is clear, put the quinces into the sirrup, cut up two oranges and mix with the quince, hang them over a gentle fire for five hours, then put them in a stone pot for use, set them in a dry cool place.

For preserving Quinces in Loaf Sugar.

Take a peck of Quinces, put them into a kettle of cold water, hang them over the fire, boil them till they are soft, then take them out with a fork, when cold, pair them, quarter or halve them, if you like; take their weight of loaf sugar, put into a bell-metal kettle or sauce pan, with one quart of water, scald and skim it till it is very clear, then put in your Quinces, let them boil in the sirrup for half an hour, add oranges as before if you like, then put them in stone pots for use.

For preserving Strawberries.

Take two quarts of Strawberries, squeeze them through a cloth, add half a pint of water and two pound of sugar, put it into a sauce pan, scald and skim it, take two pound of Strawberries with stems on, set your sauce pan on a chaffing dish, put as many Strawberries into the dish as you can with the stems up without bruizing them, let them boil for about ten minutes, then take them out gently with a fork and put them into a stone pot for use; when you have done the whole turn the sirrup into the pot, when hot; set them in a cool place for use.

Currants and Cherries may be done in the same way, by adding a little more sugar.

The American Citron.

Take the rine of a large watermelon not too ripe, cut it into small pieces, take two pound of loaf sugar, one pint of water, put it all into a ketfle, let it boil gently for four hours, then put it into pots for use.

To keep White Bullace, Pears, Plumbs, or Damsons, &c. for tarts or pies.

Gather them when full grown, and just as they begin to turn, pick all the largest out, save about two thirds of the fruit, to the other third put as much water as you think will cover them, boil and skim them; when the fruit is boiled very soft, strain it through a coarse hair sieve; and to every quart of this liquor put a pound and a half of sugar, boil it, and skim it very well; then throw in your fruit, just give them a scald; take them off the fire, and when cold, put them into bottles with wide mouths, pour your sirrup over them, lay a piece of white paper over them, and cover them with oil.

To make Marmalade.

To two pounds of quinces, put three quarters of a pound of sugar and a pint of springwater; then put them over the fire, and boil them till they are tender; then take them up and bruize them; then put them into the liquor, let it boil three quarters of an hour, and then put it into your pots or saucers.

To preserve Mulberries whole.

Set some mulberries over the fire in a skillet or preserving pan; draw from them a pint of juice when it is strained; then take three pounds of sugar beaten very fine, wet the sugar with the pint of juice, boil up your sugar and skim it, put in two pounds of ripe mulberries, and let them stand in the sirrup till they are thoroughly warm, then set them on the fire, and let them boil very gently; do them but half enough, so put them by in the sirrup till next day, then boil them gently again: when the sirrup is pretty thick, and will stand in round drops when it is cold, they are done enough, so put all into a gallipot for use.

To preserve Goosberries, Damsons, or Plumbs.

Gather them when dry, full grown, and not ripe; pick them one by one, put them into glass bottles that are very clean and dry, and cork them close with new corks; then put a kettle of water on the fire, and put in the bottles with care; wet not the corks, but let the water come up to the necks; make a gentle fire till they are a little codled and turn white; do not take them up till cold, then pitch the corks all over, or wax them close and thick; then set them in a cool dry cellar.

To preserve Peaches.

Put your peaches in boiling water, just give them a scald, but don't let them boil, take them out, and put them in cold water, then dry them in a sieve, and put them in long wide mouthed bottles: to half a dozen peaches take a quarter of a pound of sugar, clarify it, pour it over your peaches, and fill the bottles with brandy, stop them close, and keep them in a close place.

To preserve Apricots.

Take your apricots and pare them, then stone what you can whole; give them a light boiling in a pint of water, or according to your quantity of fruit; then take the weight of your apricots in sugar, and take the liquor which you boil them in, and your sugar, and boil it till it comes to a sirrup, and give them a light boiling, taking of the scum as it rises; when the sirrup jellies, it is enough; then take up the apricots, and cover them with the jelly, and put cut paper over them, and lay them down when cold. Or, take you plumbs before they have stones in them, which you may know by putting a pin through them, then codle them in many waters, till they are as green as grass; peel them and codle them again; you must take the weight of them in sugar and make a sirrup; put to your sugar a pint of water; then put them in, set them on the fire to boil slowly, till

they be clear, skimming them often, and they will be
very green. Put them up in glasses, and keep them
for use,

To preserve Cherries.

Take two pounds of cherries, one pound and a
half of sugar, half a pint of fair water, melt some sugar in it; when it is melted, put in your other sugar
and your cherries; then boil them softly, till all the
sugar be melted; then boil them fast, and skim
them; take them off two or three times and shake
them, and put them on again, and let them boil fast;
and when they are of a good colour, and the sirrup
will stand, they are boiled enough.

To preserve Raspberries.

Chuse raspberries that are not too ripe, and take the
weight of them in sugar, wet your sugar with a little
water, and put in your berries, and let them boil softly; take heed of breaking them; when they are
clear, take them up, and boil the sirrup till it be thick
enough, then put them in again; and when they are
cold, put them up in glasses.

To preserve Currants.

Take the weight of the currants in sugar, pick out
the seeds; take to a pound of sugar, half a pint of water, let it melt; then put in your currants and let
them do very leisurely, skim them, and take them up,
let the sirrup boil; then put them on again; and
when they are clear, and the sirrup thick enough,
take them off; and when they are cold, put them up
in glasses.

To preserve Plumbs.

Take your plumbs before they have stones in them,
which you may know by putting a pin through them,
then codle them in many waters till they are as
green as grass, peel them and coddle them again;
you must take the weight of them in sugar, a pint of
water, then put them in, set them on the fire, to boil
slowly till they be clear, skiming them often, and they

will be very green; put them up in glaſſes and keep them for uſe.

To keep Damſons.

Take damſons when they are firſt ripe, pick them off carefully, wipe them clean, put them into ſnuff bottles, ſtop them up tight ſo that no air can get to them, nor water; put nothing into the bottles but plumbs, put the bottles into cold water, hang them over the fire, let them heat ſlowly, let the water boil ſlowly for half an hour, when the water is cold take out the bottles, ſet the bottles into a cold place, they will keep twelve months if the bottles are ſtopped tight, ſo as no air nor water can get to them. They will not keep long after the bottles are opened; the plumbs muſt be hard.

Currant Jelly.

Having ſtripped the currants from the ſtalks, put them in a ſtone jar, ſtop it cloſe, ſet it in a kettle of boiling water, half way the jar, let it boil half an hour, take it cut and ſtrain the juice through a coarſe hair ſieve, to a pint of juice put a pound of ſugar, ſet it over a fine quick fire in a preſerving pan, or a bell-metal ſkillet, keep ſtiring it all the time till the ſugar be melted, then ſkim the ſkum off as faſt as it riſes. When the jelly is very clear and fine, pour it into earthern or china cups, when cold, cut white papers juſt the bigneſs of the top of the pot, and lay on the jelly, dip thoſe papers in brandy, then cover the top of the pot and prick it full of holes, ſet it in a dry place; you may put ſome into glaſſes for preſent uſe.

To dry Peaches.

Take the faireſt and ripeſt peaches, pare them into fair water; take their weight in double refined ſugar; of one half make a very thin ſirrup; then put in your peaches, boiling them till they look clear, then ſplit and ſtone them, boil them till they are very tender, lay them a draining, take the other half of the ſugar, and boil it almoſt to a candy; then put in your peaches, and let them lie all night then lay them on a glafs, and fet them in a ftove, till they are dry, if they are fugared too much, wipe them with a wet cloth a little; let the firft firrup be very thin, a quart of water to a pound of fugar.

To pickle or make Mangoes of Melons.

Take green melons, as many as you pleafe, and make a brine ftrong enough to bear an egg; then pour it boiling hot on the melons, keeping them down under the brine; let them ftand five or fix days; then take them out, flit them down on one fide, take out all the feeds, fcrape them well in the infide, and wafh them clean with cold water; then take a clove of a garlick, a little ginger and nutmeg fliced, and a little whole pepper; put all thefe proportionably into the melons, filling them up with muftard-feeds; then lay them in an earthern pot with the flit upwards, and take one part of muftard and two parts of vinegar, enough to cover them, pouring it upon them fcalding hot, and keep them clofe ftopped.

To pickle Barberries.

Take of white wine vinegar and water, of each an equal quantity; to every quart of this liquor, put in half a pound of cheap fugar, then pick the worft of your barberries and put into this liquor, and the beft into glaffes; then boil your pickle with the worft of your barberries, and fkim it very clean, boil it till it looks of a fine colour, then let it ftand to be cold, before you ftrain it; then ftrain it through a cloth, wringing it to get all the colour you can from the barberries; let it ftand to cool and fettle, then pour it clear into the glaffes; in a little of the pickle, boil a little fennel; when cold, put a little bit at the top of the pot or glafs, and cover it clofe with a bladder or leather. To every half pound of fugar, put a quarter of a pound of white falt.

To pickle Cucumbers.

Let your cucumbers be fmall, frefh gathered, and free from fpots; then make a pickle of falt and water, ftrong enough to bear an egg; boil the pickle and skim it well, and then pour it upon your cucumbers, and stive them down for twenty four hours; then strain them out into a cullender, and dry them well with a cloth, and take the best white wine vinegar, with cloves, sliced mace, nutmeg, white pepper corns, long pepper, and races of ginger, (as much as you please) boil them up together, and then clap the cucumbers in, with a few vine leaves, and a little salt, and as soon as they begin to turn their colour, put them into jars, stive them down close, and when cold, tie on a bladder and leather.

Alamode Beef.

Take a round of beef, and stuff it with half pound pork, half pound of butter, the soft of half a loaf of wheat bread, boil four eggs very hard, chop them up; add sweet majoram, sage, parsley, summersavory, and one ounce of cloves pounded, chop them all together, with two eggs very fine, and add a jill of wine, season very high with salt and pepper, cut holes in your beef, to put your stuffing in, then stick whole cloves into the beef, then put it into a two pail pot, with sticks at the bottom, if you wish to have the beef round when done, put it into a cloth and bind it tight with 20 or 30 yards of twine, put it into your pot with two or three quarts of water, and one jill of wine, if the round be large it will take three or four hours to bake it.

For dressing Codfish.

Put the fish first into cold water and wash it, then hang it over the fire and soak it six hours in scalding water, then shift it into clean warm water, and let it scald for one hour, it will be much better than to boil.

To boil all kinds of Garden Stuff.

In dressing all sorts of kitchen garden herbs, take care they are clean washed; that there be no small snails, or caterpillars between the leaves; and that all the coarse outer leaves, and the tops that have received any injury by the weather, be taken off; next wash them in a good deal of water, and put them into a cullender to drain, care must likewise be taken, that your pot or fauce pan be clean, well tinned, and free from fand, or greafe.

To keep Green Peas till Chrifmas.

Take young peas, fhell them, put them in a cullender to drain, then lay a cloth four or five times double on a table, then fpread them on, dry them very well, and have your bottles ready, fill them, cover them with mutton fuet fat when it is a little foft; fill the necks almoft to the top, cork them, tie a bladder and a leather over them and fet them in a dry cool place.

To boil French Beans.

Take your beans and ftring them, cut in two and then acrofs, when you have done them all, fprinkle them over with falt, ftir them together, as foon as your water boils put them in and make them boil up quick, they will be foon done and they will look of a better green than when growing in the garden if; they are very young, only break off the ends, them break in two and drefs them in the fame manner.

To boil broad Beans.

Beans require a great deal of water and it is not beft to fhell them till juft before they are ready to go into the pot, when the water boils put them in with fome picked parfley and fome falt, make them boil up quick, when you fee them begin to fall, they are done enough, ftrain them off, garnifh the difh with boiled parfley and fend plain butter in a cup or boat.

To boil green Peas.

When your peas are fhelled and the water boils which fhould not be much more than will cover them, put them in with a few leaves of mint, as foon as they boil put in a piece of butter as big as a walnut, and ftir them about, when they are done enough, ftrain them off, and fprinkle in a little falt, fhake them till the water drains off, fend them hot to the table with melted butter in a cup or boat.

To boil Afparagus.

Firft cut the white ends off about fix inches from

the head, and fcrape them from the green part down-ward very clean, as you fcrape them, throw them in-to a pan of clear water, and after a little foaking, tie them up in fmall even bundles, when your water boils, put them in, and boil them up quick ; but by over boiling they will lofe their heads ; cut a flice of bread, for a toaft, and toaft it brown on both fides ; when your afparagus is done, take it up carefully ; dip the toaft in the afparagus water, and lay it in the bottom of your difh ; then lay the heads of the afparagus on it, with the white ends outwards; pour a little melted butter over the heads; cut an orange into fmall pieces, and ftick them between for garnifh.

To boil Cabbage.

If your cabbage is large, cut it into quarters ; if fmall, cut it in halves ; let your water boil, then put in a little falt, and next your cabbage with a little more falt upon it ; make your water boil as foon as poffible, and when the ftalk is tender, take up your cabbage into a cullender, or fieve, that the water may drain off, and fend it to table as hot as you can. Savoys are dreffed in the fame manner.

For brewing Spruce Beer.

Take four ounces of hops, let them boil half an hour in one gallon of water, ftrain the hop water then add fixteen gallons of warm water, two gallons of molaffes, eight ounces of effence of fpruce, diffol-ved in one quart of water, put it in a clean cafk, then fhake it well together, add half a pint of emptins, then let it ftand and work one week, if very warm weather lefs time will do, when it is drawn off to bot-tle, add one fpoonful of molaffes to every bottle.

Emptins.

Take a handful of hops and about three quarts of water, let it boil about fifteen minutes, then make a thickening as you do for ftarch, ftrain the liquor, when cold put a little emptins to work them, they will keep well cork'd in a botttle five or fix weeks.

ADVERTISEMENT.

☞ THE author of the American Cookery, not having an education sufficient to prepare the work for the press, the person that was employed by her, and entrusted with the receipts, to prepare them for publication, (with a design to impose on her, and injure the sale of the book) did omit several articles very essential in some of the receipts, and placed others in their stead, which were highly injurious to them, without her consent—which was unknown to her, till after publication ; but she has removed them as far as possible, by the following

ERRATA.

Page 25. Rice pudding, No. 2 ; for one pound butter, read half pound—for 14 eggs read 8. No. 5 ; after half pint rice, add 6 ounces sugar.

Page 26. A nice Indian pudding, No. 3 ; boil only 6 hours.—A flour pudding ; read 9 spoons of flour, put in scalding milk ; bake an hour and half.—A boiled flour pudding ; 9 spoons of flour, boil an hour and half.

Page 27. A cream almond pudding ; for 8 yolks and 3 whites, read 8 eggs ; for 1 spoon flour, read 8—boil an hour and half.

Potatoe pudding, No. 1, No. 2. add a pint flour to each.

Page 29. Puff pastes for tarts, No, 3 ; for 12 eggs read 6.

Page 33. Plain cake ; for 1 quart of emptins, read 1 pint.

Page 35. Another plain cake, No. 5 ; for 9 pounds of flour, read 18 pounds.

In all Puddings, where cream is mentioned, milk may be used.

In Pastes, the white of eggs only are to be used.